The Coffee Club

George Boundy

ISBN-13: 978-1-7239-8481-5

CONTENTS

COFFEE CLUB #1

Layer on Layer on Layer of foam.

Steam the milk, the mist rises.

First sip at what lay beneath.

I feel my courage stir.

The mire of cars and horns and air-con

Fade away as the cup empties.

A storm begins to rumble underneath.

I look and you are there.

This is not an official club.

There are no memberships.

Yet every Wednesday we meet to stare

At the cup pressed to our lips.

We do not talk of coffee,

Caffeine or the rush.

We never even talked at all

Until that time you borrowed my brush.

You didn't need to fix your hair,

It was perfect as it was.

As perfect as it always is,

Like crema on the top.

The cup begins to cool, as the best bits are behind us.

The rush, the thrill, the waking up.

We finish the coffee, though we know

It will never be as good as it was.

We are Froogle.

It cost us £4.90.

You turn left at the door

I turn right.

We'd kiss if it weren't for the coffee,

But if it weren't for the coffee we'd have never had the chance.

A final fleeting glance.

.

DARK ROAST

Blacker than the night's sky

And thicker than the sea.

I swell beneath your warm embrace,

You capture me: I am free.

Smoke as full as feather pillows

And drier than course sand.

I expand as I breathe in you deep.

I falter; take my hand.

A lighter note emerges.

Through the ebony expanse,

My every moment is drawn to you

And you'd kill if you had the chance.

They say they always knew your darkness,

But I only saw the light.

I lived in happy cloudless days

You lived always under night.

There is a kind of beauty

To the darker times of life.

Yet when you finally slipped away

I was not bathed in light.

I feel that darkness with me still.

That bitter pile of dust.

I think perhaps your first mistake

Was learning not to trust.

Blacker than the night's sky

And thicker that the sea.

I am the darkness now that you

Will never return to me.

FULL-CAFF

1 cup, 2 cup, 3 cup, 4

Perhaps I shouldn't,

But I'd like some more!

5 cup, 6 cup, 7 cup, 8

Just one more then,

Sorry I was late.

9 cup, 10 cup, 11 cup, 12

The store is closing,

They ring the bell.

The day should end with one final cup,

But 13's unlucky, 14 brings luck!

Just before bed, a round 15.

It divides by 5, and divides by 3.

This caffeine has given me all that I need.

Until I need more, once I run out of speed.

DE-CAFF

Is this what childhood felt like?

Before I learned to like the taste.

I can't believe it felt this way,

If it had, I wouldn't have grown up.

Is this what mindfulness feels like?

The constant knowing about what's going on,

No constant blanket of haze.

I like that blanket. It's mine.

Is this what living feels like?

I thought I'd been living a while now.

But I've never lived like this.

Who would?

Is this what it feels like to die?

The quiet embers fizzling out.

The sense of knowing that it's not all bad.

Even if it is.

Is this what other people feel?

If it is then I pity them more.

I shouldn't wonder why people suffer,

When their life is an endless bore.

Is this what the puritan's felt like?

Did it bring them closer to God?

Hell has opened and the devils are here.

I've kept them back quite well until now.

Is this what it feels like to go into space?

To look back at the world you have left,

And wonder why you were so keen

On it the first place?

Is this how King Midas felt?

When he sat in his tomb of gold,

Unable to touch but surrounded by so much.

Is that why I feel alone?

Is this what it feels like to go on a diet?

Ignore all the noise, to sit in quiet.

Well, as I guess you can tell,

There's a noise inside I just can't quell.

FAIRTRADE™

There once was a man who farmed coffee

Which he sold for the price of a toffee,

But his labours were hard,

His hands they were scared.

And his legs were as weak as banoffee.

Then came a man from the west

Sunburned all over his chest,

That said he'd trade fair,

Split the profits to spare,

And with that they both could invest.

Now the farmer thought what he could do,

If what this man said could be true,

Send his children to college,

Eat more than plain porridge.

And for him no more, 'mend and make do.'

There once was a man who farmed coffee,

Which he sold through third parties by proxy,

Now that trading was fair

He could live without care,

Or at least he can still grow your coffee.

CAFETIERE

I see a swamp, a throbbing bloom of inky moss.

There is some potent smell,

Aroma where I dwell.

The smoke of creation percolates

Around the void, above

A blackened sky, a single white dove.

Amidst this chaos, nowhere land

A steel Pilar stands,

Slips under ancient sands.

A bubble pops abreast this world,

The Oceans are become.

The world is now begun.

Slowly the crust of the swamp peels away,

One vast and lonely lake,

Are we God's mistake?

The steel rod descends further still.

Leaves behind delusion,

New world infusion.

At last the lake is amber-brown.

I dip my lips to taste.

I paddle to my waist.

The lake is bordered by walls of glass.

Who is that looking in?

Is this original sin?

My world upends itself. The lake pours out.

Libations to my lord.

I wonder what it's for.

I see the rod was connected to

A plate with many holes.

Beneath are long-dead souls.

Is this the fate of all our race?

To give all that we've got,

Then dwell among the rot?

The swamp will now be emptied out,

The whole process repeated.

I'm still here, undefeated.

INSTANT

"When shall we three meet again?"

Next Wednesday, round at mine.

ORGANIC

I'm still not sure how the ladies met,

But they come here three times a week.

Their make-up impeccable, their hair well-set.

Ruby-red blush on each cheek.

The ladies natter over the din

And I hear of what their sons do.

One lives in Stansted, one lives in sin,

With a man down in Kathmandu.

Their faces tell a thousand plots

Yet the perfume hides it well.

One of them wears bright green culottes

Another, a star-spangled veil.

The lady who seems to be in charge,

beckons me with a click.

She looks me over, her eyes at large

And asks for a latté, 'thanks chick.'

They are each other's safety net,

Each secret a special trinket.

They owe each other a mighty debt,

I fill their cup, they drink it.

They have grown old together,

Ever since they were small,

I hope one day I'll be like them,

They talk to me: I hear age call.

ESPRESSO

Rest here a while.

Tell me secrets you can't keep.

Gossip fills the air.

18

COFFEE CLUB #2

Subscription comes at a premium now,

Our little club has grown.

There's people talking about the drink,

Shudder to think how.

They put a table out for us now,

That used to sit out the back.

It makes one appreciate,

All the love and the hate

Between your fellow man.

Or woman.

We're further from each other now,

As founders we need to be impartial.

We need to show them the way,

To read the Sermon on the Mount

And principally, to count

How many Americano's that was.

In truth our temple is but a cog,

We clog the machine, which they soon fix.

With one swift wipe and a purging hiss,

All sin is behind us, all memory of that kiss.

It might just be the caffeine talking,

But I swear the prices are going up.

It's now £6 for a simple cup.

What is it but burnt bake beans?

One neophyte boldly asks.

I smile and he smiles back,

Knowing only too well,

What the answer was.

CAPPUCCINO

He said we'd go for one quick drink

I've had mine and he isn't here

The froth still holds a cameo

Of his face: my unknown Romeo

The Barista tries not to stare

I watch the clock and blink.

He texts me that he's stuck in a meeting

I order another, just for the taste

This time he draws a simple flower

A quick drink now that lasts an hour

Sipped and supped without haste

Languish in this moment, fleeting.

He asks if we can skip the date

I lick the final spoon of foam

The Barista hands me a paper napkin

The promise of sheets soon to be wrapped in

His name and number, on their own

He finishes after half past eight.

ICED LATTÉ

The chill slides down my throat like winter morning frost.

They close the door behind them.

I thought last night the hardest thing was living with the cost.

I am whizzed up indecision.

It glides into the room like the promised milk and honey,

Is this what we wanted?

It is trivial now in the cold light of day to think of money.

I divide into light and dark.

My love has left the coffee club

And turned to pastures new.

I wander what the future holds

What am I to do?

LOYALTY

Those points he accrued are sitting,

Waiting to be used.

I am waiting too,

And not for the first time.

A large latté hangs in the air

Like a cat, neither dead not alive.

I thrive on his appearance.

I need it.

One time, under some duress

He couldn't find the card

Gave me his address

And balance was restored.

I remember that.

Does this mean he doesn't want that I have to give?

The green, green grass is greener over there?

Should I even care?

He's the one who's missing out

I shout.

They stare.

Another few points and he could have a pastry.

He's intolerant to gluten but it's the thought that counts.

I picture each sweet ounce.

The bit that hurts the most is not that he strayed

But that he stayed

Away.

If he came back, what would I say?

Welcome home oh picture perfect man

This is your latté

Sip it down, slow as you can.

Steep me in it.

Take the weight off your weary feet.

Walking to the other side of the street

Must have taken its toll.

You said you were out for a stroll.

But you're back now, where you belong.

I still remember your favourite song.

The one by that woman who died suddenly.

I'll sing it too you softly.

"Take me, to the coconut tree.

That's where my heart is

Under its leaves.

"Take me, as far as you'll go.

I don't want nothin'

You reap what you sow.

"Take me, to the coconut tree

When all the clouds are fallin'

Down on me"

But you're not here, under cloudless skies,

You're not here, where your loyalty lies.

MR. BARISTA

They come and go like the ebb and flow of a tidal lock,

Run amok, then slowly fade away.

I am their constant, always there, they're the ones that rise and leave.

New leaves shooting on the trees outside.

I glide through the orders, surfing on foam.

Searching for some kind of connection I make a simple flower.

A Daisy, like my grandmother.

The coco, milk and coffee mix

A floral eclipse,

A moment, a breath.

Taking the cup I present it with two hands,

No sign of a wedding band,

He smiles through tears.

In years and years we will muse on how we met and tell

Our grandchildren that well.

It was written in the stars.

Then the phone bleeps,

Apprehension leaps and I leave him.

Taking up my ballpoint pen,

Black and nearly out of ink.

I think on how I've never done this before, but always wanted to.

In the days to come it will seem quite crass,

How we walked out of that place, your hand upon my ass.

But in that moment it was almost perfect.

I felt in that moment like caramel,

Dripping from a fresh pump.

When we reach the seven year slump

I'll remember that and grin.

"This is a sin," my younger self begins.

"This is right," my heart replies.

He will become my love, my Mr.

Mr Barista, you and I.

He'll make the coffee, and I'll stand by.

And we'll know that this is right.

COFFEE CLUB #3

They now serve Salad here,

And it's really not the same.

Did you know that salad is derived from an Arabic world for Salt?

Salted things?

He would have known.

He would have filled it in.

4 down, A thing comes from Turkish salt (5).

I want pastry and custard and jam

Not this green thing, an egg, a sliver of Ham.

I want the old gang back together,

And yet I am alone.

I sit in the corner,

The table long gone,

Back out back, where it belongs.

My one regret was not making it clear

I tried but my tongue furred up with fear.

I take milk now, and two white sugars

Because what is the point in anything else?

The club disbanded before it's time,

Like all the good boy bands did.

The truth that all of us had the chance,

But none of us hand the balls.

Glitter baubles hang from the tree outside.

He would have hated that, before he died.

ABOUT THE AUTHOR

George Boundy grew up in Essex and trained as an Actor at East 15 Acting School before gaining a Master's Degree in Playwriting Studies from The University of Birmingham. His prime companion is most likely his Dachshund Chummy.

Printed in Great Britain
by Amazon

84039032R00021